INSIDE THE
TOBACCO INDUSTRY

by Tom Streissguth

Content Consultant

Dr. Barbara Hahn

Associate Professor of History
Texas Tech University

BIG
BUSINESS

Essential Library

An Imprint of Abdo Publishing | abdopublishing.com

abdopublishing.com

Published by Abdo Publishing, a division of ABDO, PO Box 398166, Minneapolis, Minnesota 55439. Copyright © 2017 by Abdo Consulting Group, Inc. International copyrights reserved in all countries. No part of this book may be reproduced in any form without written permission from the publisher. Essential Library™ is a trademark and logo of Abdo Publishing.

Printed in the United States of America, North Mankato, Minnesota
102016
012017

Cover Image: Wanvinai Samsee/Shutterstock Images
Interior Photos: Shutterstock Images, 4, 8; Owen Humphreys/PA Wire/AP Images, 10–11; akg-images/SuperStock, 12; Morphart Creation/Shutterstock Images, 15; Universal History Archive/UGI/Getty Images, 16, 44; Stapleton Historical Collection/Heritage Images/Glow Images, 21; Pictorial Press Ltd/Alamy, 23; Zbigniew Guzowski/Shutterstock Images, 24; CrackerClips Stock Media/Shutterstock Images, 26; Curved Light USA/Alamy, 30–31; Everett Historical/Shutterstock Images, 34, 48, 50; Buyenlarge/Archive Photos/Getty Images, 37; Lewis W. Hine/Library of Congress, 39; Harris & Ewing/Library of Congress, 41; Sputnik/Alamy, 43; B. Christopher/Alamy, 52; Red Line Editorial, 54–55, 96–97; Underwood Photo Archives/SuperStock, 56; Robert Landau/Corbis Historical/Getty Images, 59; Fritz Gotto/The LIFE Picture Collection/Getty Images, 61; SuperStock/Glow Images, 64; Apic/Hulton Archive/Getty Images, 66; S. K. Howard/iStockphoto, 69; Dirck Halstead/The LIFE Images Collection/Getty Images, 73; Frances M. Roberts/Newscom, 75; Bettmann/Getty Images, 76; Arno Burgi/picture-alliance/dpa/AP Images, 81; Richard Hartog/Los Angeles Times/Getty Images, 83; Rob Hainer/Shutterstock Images, 86; Rich Pedroncelli/AP Images, 90–91; Wolfram Steinberg/picture-alliance/dpa/AP Images, 93; Kyodo/AP Images, 94

Editor: Tracey Dils
Series Designer: Craig Hinton

Publisher's Cataloging-in-Publication Data

Names: Streissguth, Tom, author.
Title: Inside the tobacco industry / by Tom Streissguth.
Description: Minneapolis, MN : Abdo Publishing, 2017. | Series: Big business |
    Includes bibliographical references and index.
Identifiers: LCCN 2016945205 | ISBN 9781680783759 (lib. bdg.) |
    ISBN 9781680797282 (ebook)
Subjects: LCSH: Tobacco industry--Juvenile literature. | Tobacco products--
    Juvenile literature.
Classification: DDC 338.4--dc23
LC record available at http://lccn.loc.gov/2016945205

Contents

1 | TOBACCO AND NICOTINE

Daniel Walsh worked hard, on some days for almost 20 hours. A scientist, he worked on artificial intelligence software and products in San Francisco, California. He also craved tobacco. Try as he might, he couldn't give up cigarettes. Then Walsh learned about something new: the electronic cigarette. Often called e-cigarettes, these smoking devices look like regular cigarettes. However, e-cigarettes, or e-cigs, are battery powered and produce vapor rather than smoke. Similar to traditional cigarettes, they contain nicotine, a chemical that is highly addictive.

Many cigarette smokers who were hooked on nicotine were switching to e-cigs. Trying to stop his tobacco use, Walsh also made the change. The switch proved so successful that Walsh realized he was onto something big, and he left the high-tech industry. He moved to Gaylord, Michigan, and launched Purebacco. This company makes e-liquids that go into e-cigarettes. Purebacco has grown into a successful enterprise, with 30 employees. In 2014, the company made 2,400 gallons (9,000 L) of e-liquid, selling its products in more than 700 retail outlets.[1] Walsh built an expensive research lab to develop new flavors. He discovered nicotine-delivery systems can also deliver big profits.

E-cigarettes are a popular way for cigarette smokers to reduce the amount of nicotine they consume.

The tobacco industry has been growing for more than 300 years. From its birthplace in North America, it has spread around the world. Some companies that make cigarettes, cigars, and pipe tobacco may see e-cigarettes as a threat to their business. Others are adapting, making their own products for those who want to make the switch.

EARLY TOBACCO

For the native people of the Americas, tobacco was an important plant. The dried leaves of the tobacco plant made a popular gift. In some cultures, smoking a pipe was thought to bring peace among individuals and tribes. Some believed an offering of tobacco assured a good harvest and calm weather. The smoke of a tobacco pipe was believed to carry human thoughts and visions. This connected those who smoked tobacco with the world of the spirits.

American Indians from different cultural traditions consumed tobacco in various ways. They smoked the leaves or ground them into a powder to inhale through the nose. They chewed tobacco, drank it as a tea, or simply ate it. Tobacco smoke was used to get rid of crop pests, and tobacco juice cleansed the body of lice. Tobacco was also effective against toothaches, headaches, wounds, and snakebites. It was involved in some rites of initiation. A young person's first experience with tobacco represented a passage to adulthood in some tribes.

TOBACCO SCIENCE

Tobacco originated in the Western Hemisphere. Today, the plant has spread all over the world. The *Nicotiana tabacum* plant, commonly known as tobacco, grows approximately five feet (1.5 m) high.

It produces several broad and flat leaves that grow from a thick stem. The tobacco plant belongs to the genus *Nicotiana*. The plants in this genus feature tubular or trumpet-shaped flowers.

When smoked, tobacco causes physical changes in the smoker, including raised blood pressure and a faster heart rate, dizziness, and sweating. Tobacco smoke works as a stimulant in small doses or serves as a depressant when inhaled deeply and taken in larger doses. The nicotine in tobacco is the source of its effects on the human body. In pure form nicotine can be lethal. This makes it a useful ingredient in insecticides. When combined with other ingredients in the tobacco leaf, it has milder effects on humans.

N. tabacum and *N. rustica* were the two varieties cultivated in North America at the time of Christopher Columbus's arrival from Europe in 1492. Today, *N. tabacum* is grown for smoking and chewing. *N. rustica*, or wild tobacco, is not widely produced for human consumption.

A BIG BUSINESS

Over time, tobacco smoking was taken up by new European arrivals in North America. Their descendants built tobacco growing into an important farm industry. Eventually, tobacco

Tobacco Self-Defense

To fight insect pests, tobacco plants evolved to produce nicotine as a powerful defense mechanism. This compound is fatal to most insects that eat tobacco leaves. Scientists have also discovered that when eaten by tobacco hornworm caterpillars, tobacco plants release chemicals known as green leaf volatiles. These produce a smell that acts like a distress call, attracting species that love to eat the eggs and larvae of these caterpillars.

Tobacco plants are grown for their leaves, so the plants' flowers are usually removed and discarded.

developed into a multinational business, profitable for companies large and small.

Tobacco is a leisure product. It's not essential for survival, as many other farm commodities are, nor is it useful for economic sectors such as communication, transportation, education, or shelter. This means tobacco companies must somehow create a demand for their product. Companies achieve this goal through advertising that associates cigarettes and other tobacco products with relaxation, glamour, and fun. The history of the tobacco business parallels the rise of mass marketing in the United States and other countries. In many ways, tobacco

A Taxing Debate

After winning its independence in 1783, the United States had to raise revenue. There was no tax on income, so money had to be raised through other means, including excise taxes. Congress debated a tax on tobacco, but Founding Father and future president James Madison strongly opposed it, saying:

> As to the subject before the House, it was proper to choose taxes the least unequal. Tobacco excise was a burden the most unequal. It fell upon the poor, upon the sailors, day-laborers, and other people of these

Sin taxes, or excise taxes on items deemed socially undesirable, became more common through the 1800s. Tobacco joined these items after the American Civil War (1861–1865). By 2016, the US government was taxing cigarettes, cigars, chewing tobacco, snuff, pipe tobacco, and cigarette papers, collecting approximately $12 billion a year in taxes on these tobacco products.[3]

companies pioneered this important business art.

Yet tobacco also has negative publicity. Cigarettes, pipe tobacco, and cigars are linked to cancer, heart disease, and other deadly illnesses. Health researchers are certain: smoking can kill. Consumers who suffered the consequences of smoking have brought lawsuits against tobacco companies and won billions of dollars in settlements and court judgments. The rate of smoking among adults has steadily fallen, starting in the late 1900s. While this may seem to be bad news for tobacco companies, they remain profitable, and their products are still in high demand around the world.

2 | TOBACCO IN THE COLONIES

Italian explorer Christopher Columbus arrived at the island of San Salvador in the Bahamas in 1492, claiming the land on behalf of the monarchs of Spain. The first party of native Taino people who came to meet Columbus offered tobacco as a gift. Not knowing what to make of the strange dried leaves, the crew of Columbus's ship threw them overboard. While the navigator explored the island of Cuba, two members of his party, Rodrigo de Jerez and Luis de Torres, became the first Europeans to smoke tobacco. Fra Bartolomé de las Casas, who owned a copy of Columbus's ship log, told the story of this encounter in 1514:

> These two Christians met many people on the road, men and women, and the men
> always with a firebrand in their hands, and certain herbs to take their smokes which are
> some dried herbs, put in a certain leaf, dry also, after the fashion of a musket made
> of paper . . . lit at one end and at the other they chew or suck and take in
> with their breath that smoke which dulls their flesh and as it were
> intoxicates and so they say that they do not feel weariness.
> Those muskets or whatever we call them they call
> tobacos.[1]

Columbus's relations with the indigenous people of the Americas began peacefully, but the conqueror would soon begin destroying the societies he encountered.

ARRIVAL IN EUROPE

After Columbus, more European explorers arrived in North America. They returned home with tobacco. Francisco Hernandez de Toledo brought the first tobacco plants to Spain in 1510. In 1560, Jean Nicot de Villemain, the French ambassador to Portugal, sent tobacco plants from Brazil to the king of France. He also offered powdered tobacco, or snuff, to Queen Catherine de Medici as a cure for migraine headaches. Sir Walter Raleigh popularized tobacco in England in the late 1500s. Raleigh was the first to use a clay pipe to smoke dried and crushed tobacco leaves.

Tobacco smoking caught on quickly in Europe. In France, the tobacco plant was named *nicotina*, in honor of Jean Nicot. Smokers used clay pipes or cigars—dried tobacco rolled into a tobacco leaf. But the smoke was too harsh and strong to inhale into the lungs. Before cigarettes, tobacco smokers circulated the smoke through the mouth and nose, and then exhaled.

Tobacco was rare and expensive, and smoking cigars or using tobacco pipes was a habit only for those who could afford it. The less-wealthy people

Tobacco and Health

Long before modern cancer studies, many people believed in the health benefits of chewing or smoking tobacco. When it arrived in Europe, traders claimed tobacco could cure toothaches and headaches. But modern medicine has changed its mind on these prescriptions. Smoking actually causes the blood vessels to constrict and the nerves in the back of the throat to narrow, worsening headaches. The habit also causes cancer in the lungs and elsewhere, is linked to heart disease and strokes, and is responsible for damage to nearly every organ in the body.

Sir Walter Raleigh visited America in 1578. Later he helped fund the colony at Roanoke, which was soon abandoned.

of Spain, however, discovered a solution. They picked up discarded cigars, shredded them, and rolled them in paper to smoke. These *papelotes* spread the habit of smoking to Portugal, Italy, and other nations of Europe. The French named the little paper cigars *cigarettes*.

The English had an appetite for tobacco as well. But the tropical plant did not flourish in the soil or the climate of the island kingdom. England would soon look to its American colonies. There, Native people had been growing tobacco successfully for thousands of years. And soon, large plantations would begin growing, harvesting, and exporting the plant in larger quantities than ever before.

In 1612, John Rolfe of the Jamestown Colony in Virginia started a tobacco plantation. In a short time, tobacco spread to other colonies and to the Caribbean region. It would become the most important cash crop grown in England's American colonies. The desire to harvest growing quantities of the lucrative crop would help spread the system of slavery throughout these agricultural regions.

Jailed for Smoking

Rodrigo de Jerez sailed on Columbus's first voyage to the New World in 1492. When he returned to Spain, Jerez brought something new: tobacco in the form of cigars. The authorities in Spain did not look kindly on this strange, smoky habit. The Inquisition, a religious court, threw Jerez in jail for seven years. When he won his freedom, Jerez discovered that smoking had since become acceptable and popular in Spain.

A CASH CROP

The tobacco trading business flourished in England. The royal court granted valuable monopolies to certain individuals to import tobacco from the colonies. The English king James I, an enemy of Sir Walter Raleigh, wrote *A Counterblaste to Tobacco*, a scathing tract on what he saw as a filthy habit:

The Cigarette Appears

Depictions of smoking go back at least 1,000 years to a Maya clay pot found in Guatemala that showed a man smoking a roll of tobacco leaves. The first work of art to depict a cigarette was *La Cometa*, a painting by the Spanish artist Francisco Goya. Completed in 1778, the painting shows a group of people watching a kite. On the ground sits a man puffing on a *papelote*. The *papelote* was the precursor to the modern cigarette.

Have you not reason then to bee ashamed, and to forbeare this filthie noveltie, so basely grounded, so foolishly received and so grossely mistaken in the right use thereof? . . . A custome lothsome to the eye, hatefull to the Nose, harmefull to the braine, dangerous to the Lungs, and in the blacke stinking fume thereof, neerest resembling the horrible Stigian smoke of the pit that is bottomelesse.[2]

For the king, tobacco smoke conjured thoughts of the biblical hell and its burning brimstone. But it also smelled like money—tax money. Instead of banning tobacco, he raised the tax on it from two pence per pound to 6 shillings, 10 pence per pound—a hike of 4,000 percent.[3] If smoking was a sinful act, then the king would place a heavy tax on sin. To limit quantity and keep the price of tobacco and revenues high, James also banned the growing of tobacco in England. Virginia and Bermuda were granted the exclusive right to export tobacco. The other rulers of Europe set their own policies toward tobacco. In Turkey, smoking in public could bring a death penalty. In Spain, tobacco commerce was limited to the city of Seville.

GROWING TOBACCO

Growing tobacco was difficult in the colonies. The tiny seeds do not survive direct planting. Instead, they have to start life in a protected, prepared bed of soil. After a few weeks of growing, the farmer could transplant the seedlings into his fields. After this, an ongoing battle began against the wide variety of weeds and insects attracted to the tobacco plant.

Paying the Price for Smoking

Antismoking laws in America go all the way back to the colony of Massachusetts. In early Massachusetts, smoking tobacco in public was a crime. The punishment was time in the stocks. The stocks were a device that holds arms and legs in place, so the convict could not walk, move, or do much of anything. The stocks were placed in a public place so that everyone could see the offender. Edwin Proon was one of the first to break the no-smoking law and suffer the consequences. When he began smoking in the stocks, local law enforcement put a stop to it by placing an iron hood over his head.

Even if a farmer successfully kept away these pests, there was still more work to do before the harvest. In a process called topping, the farmer cut away tall stalks that sapped the water from the leaves, a process called topping. Suckers, small growths that grew near the plant's base, also had to be cut. After the leaves were picked, they could not be shipped until they were cured. That meant tying the leaves in bundles and hanging them to dry in a barn or shed. To speed up the process,

A Growing Habit

Just a few years after John Rolfe planted his first crop, tobacco became Virginia's most important export to Europe. Tobacco was meeting a growing demand in the colonies themselves as well. A French visitor to North America noticed that the habit of smoking had spread to every corner of the English colonists' society:

> I sometimes went to hear the sermon; their churches are in the woods, and when everyone has arrived the minister and all the others smoke before going in. The preaching over; they do the same thing before parting. They have seats for that purpose. It was here I saw that everybody smokes, men, women, girls and boys from the age of several years.[4]

the farmer kept an open fire going. As a result of these fires, many tobacco barns burned to the ground.

Entire enslaved families were forced into the backbreaking labor of preparing tobacco.

Once cured, tobacco leaves were packed into big barrels called hogsheads. The timing of this process was critical. Tobacco farmers sold their crop at auctions, where buyers would pay higher prices for better quality. Leaves that were still too moist would easily spoil in shipment. Leaves that cured too long became too dry. They lost their flavor and were worth less.

TOBACCO AND SLAVERY

Though tobacco was originally well-suited for small family farms, as demand grew it was impossible for a single farmer, even with the help of his family, to work a large tobacco plantation. In the colonies of Virginia and Maryland in the 1600s, tobacco growers used indentured servants to work their crop. Indentured servants were brought to the

United States and, in return for free passage, were under contract to work for a specified period, usually four to seven years. After they served their time, they were released.

Slaves work in a tobacco warehouse in Richmond, Virginia.

The practice of indentured servitude gradually died out around 1700. Growers began using enslaved Africans to work the tobacco fields. The slave industry brought millions of captive Africans to the Caribbean and the United States through the middle of the 1800s. Many were put to work in the tobacco fields of Maryland and Virginia.

3 | CIGARS, CIGARETTES, AND BRANDS

In North America, as settlers moved west, they brought tobacco. After the American Revolution (1775–1783), tobacco farmers built new plantations in Virginia, Maryland, and South Carolina. Lighter and poorer soils gave rise to lighter strains of the plant. These varieties produced smoke that was easier on the throat and could be enjoyed in larger quantities. Tobacco smoking became cheaper and more prevalent among all economic levels of society.

The Spanish colony of Cuba began exporting tobacco to the United States in 1817. By a royal decree, the king of Spain allowed Cuban farmers to trade with the United States. The decree was meant to stimulate the Cuban economy, help Cuban farmers prosper, and make the island a valuable piece of the Spanish Empire. Popular among wealthy Americans, Cuban cigars gained a reputation as the best in the world. By the mid-1840s, tobacco replaced sugar as Cuba's principal crop, and by the mid-1850s, the island was home to more than 9,500 tobacco plantations and 2,000 cigar factories.[1]

New varieties of tobacco cultivated in the 1700s and 1800s helped make smoking more common.

Spittoons ranged from utilitarian to elaborately decorated.

In the United States, however, the most popular form of tobacco was chew—a small plug of dried and cured leaf. Men, women, and children used plug tobacco at all times of day, indoors and out. When excess juices filled the mouth, the user spit them out. Tobacco-stained floors were a common feature in homes and public places, and spittoons, special containers for spitting, were placed everywhere.

The habit caused English author Charles Dickens distress. Although Dickens admired many things about America, he didn't care for tobacco chewing. In his account of an 1842 trip to the United States, called *American Notes*, he wrote, "Washington [DC] may be called the head-quarters of tobacco-tinctured saliva. . . . The thing itself is an exaggeration of nastiness, which cannot be outdone."[2]

THE DISCOVERY OF BRIGHT LEAF

North Carolina had the right soil and climate for growing tobacco. But since colonial times, the state lagged behind Virginia and Maryland in the American tobacco market. Everything changed after a fateful discovery led to North Carolina's tobacco boom.

According to local legend, an enslaved man named Stephen lived and worked on a farm owned by Abisha Slade in Caswell County. A blacksmith, Stephen made and repaired iron tools and wheels. He also handled tobacco curing. One day in 1839, while watching the fire in the curing barn, he fell asleep. When he awoke, he found that the fire had nearly died out. Rushing to his blacksmith's pit, Stephen took a few hot coals to throw on the tobacco fire. A burst of heat and flame suddenly turned the tobacco a bright yellow.

The result of this accidental discovery was bright leaf tobacco, which became a North Carolina specialty. The new "flue-cured" method spread to other farms. Slade devoted his farm to tobacco, producing 20,000 pounds (9,100 kg) every year.[3] Bright leaf was easy to grow in North Carolina's sandy soils and less expensive than the flavored tobaccos sold to pipe smokers.

Sharecropping

After the Civil War, slave labor was replaced in many areas by a system known as sharecropping. Blacks, chiefly former slaves, as well as poor whites became sharecroppers. They borrowed land, living quarters, tools, seeds, and farm animals from a landowner. They grew and harvested the crop, while the landowner decided which crops to grow and managed selling the harvest. The proceeds balanced against the sharecropper's debt, but the system was rigged so the landowner could keep the laborers indebted. Tobacco, cotton, and rice were common crops grown under this system. One step up from sharecropping was tenant farming. A tenant paid rent for the use of fields and a house and owned and controlled the crops. In 1890, one-third of white farmers and three-quarters of black farmers were tenants or sharecroppers.[5]

Bright leaf was an ideal tobacco for inhaling. The lighter, less bitter smoke was easier to take into the lungs than the darker varieties used in cigars. While cigar smokers kept the smoke in their mouth and throat, cigarettes were inhaled. The acidic nature of flue-cured tobacco prevents its easy absorption in the mouth and throat.

As cigarettes gained a widespread market, the federal government began to take an interest in smoking. The government imposed a tax on cigars in July 1862 to help fund the American Civil War (1861–1865). In 1864, a separate tax on cigarettes began. The taxes were raised several times after the Civil War. Tobacco helped pay the expenses of the Spanish-American War (1898).

MASS PRODUCTION

In 1880, cigarette consumption in the United States reached 500 million cigarettes per year.[4] Hundreds of small tobacco factories operated in New York City, the capital of the cigarette business. The barriers to entry were low. A tobacco business needed only the inexpensive raw leaves, paper to roll them in, and workers to roll them.

A key challenge for cigarette makers was marketing. Since all cigarettes were basically the same, tobacco companies began creating brands to differentiate their products. Bull Durham cigarettes, produced by W. T. Blackwell of Durham, North Carolina, was the first brand to be nationally advertised. The ads, which appeared in local and regional newspapers and billboards, used a bull as a logo.

At the same time, cigarette packaging evolved. Allen & Ginter of Richmond, Virginia, began selling cigarettes bundled in wrappers with a cardboard insert. In addition to the Allen and Ginter name, these inserts displayed pictures of sports stars, historical figures, and attractive women. They were the first collectible trading cards.

The First Baseball Cards

Allen & Ginter's 1887 "World Champions" set of 50 athletes included baseball players, wrestlers, rowers, boxers, shooters, and pool players. This was the first set of color lithographs produced for cigarette packs and is now one of the most rare and valuable of all trading cards. Today, the cards can sell for more than $1,000 each.[7]

THE BONSACK MACHINE

In an era in which steam-powered machinery was changing the manufacturing world, cigarettes were still rolled by hand. This limited their production. Could a machine actually make a cigarette? To find out, Allen & Ginter offered a $75,000 prize for the first functional rolling machine.[6] A young inventor named James Bonsack took up the challenge. In March 1881, he patented a device that could make up to 212 cigarettes a minute.[8] Allen and Ginter tried the machine, but, fearing it was unreliable, they decided against using it.

Some Bull Durham advertisements on the sides of buildings are still visible today.

James "Buck" Duke of W. Duke, Sons & Co. saw the potential. He had two Bonsack machines installed in his North Carolina tobacco factory. He also hired operators to work alongside the skilled cigarette makers he had recruited from New York. For a time, the Bonsack machines worked well, and production skyrocketed. Duke leased the machines from Bonsack on favorable terms. When operating at full capacity, a single Bonsack machine could turn out 100,000 cigarettes per day, as opposed to the 2,000 per day achieved by human rollers.[9] Machines worked around the clock. They never

took breaks, they didn't complain or demand raises, and, important for Duke and other producers, they never went out on strike.

The Cigarette Opera

In 1878, New York operagoers were the first in the nation to see the opera *Carmen*, by Georges Bizet. The story of an untamed gypsy "cigarette girl" of Seville played a major role in promoting the new tobacco product to the American public. *Carmen* gave cigarettes an air of the exotic and forbidden. At the time, Catholic Spain was a rival of the United States, both culturally and politically. Anti-Catholic prejudice was strong, and *Carmen* associated smoking with defiance against conventional American values.

Carmen became one of the most popular operas in the world, but the scenes with smoking stirred up controversy. In 2014, the West Australian Opera company no longer staged the work, announcing it wanted to promote healthy habits among its audience.

UNION TROUBLE

To fight for better wages and working conditions, workers banded together in unions and appointed representatives to negotiate with company bosses. If necessary, the workers called strikes or work slowdowns to achieve their demands. Urban tobacco workers, including cigarette rollers, were among the first US workers to form unions.

Duke's employees in North Carolina were producing up to 250,000 cigarettes every day.[10] These skilled workers took pride in their speed and efficiency. They also feared the loss of their jobs. No human could match the speed of a Bonsack machine, despite its complicated mechanism and frequent breakdowns. Duke saw the Bonsack machines as the industry's future. To fight the automation of W. Duke, Sons & Co., workers formed a chapter of the Cigarmaker's Progressive Union

(CMPU). Duke agreed to lower production goals for the hand rollers, but he also kept the Bonsack machines operating.

In 1885, the CMPU voted to become exclusively a union for cigar makers. Some of Duke's workers tried to join another union, the Knights of Labor, but the company threatened to fire any employee who joined. Eventually, Duke instituted automated cigarette making in his factories.

Duke worked hard to promote his brands, creating an enormous demand for the product. He spent large amounts of money on advertising and made special deals with retail outlets to undercut his competitors' sales. He inserted coupons into cigarette packs for customers. To attract the largely male market for cigarettes, he put images of women on his cigarette cards. By the 1890s, W. Duke, Sons & Co. was producing and selling 2 million cigarettes every day.[11] The Bonsack machines made cigarettes even cheaper to produce. For a time, Duke sold his cigarettes at a loss to drive his competitors out of business. Eventually, despite the low price of its products, the company made enormous profits. It bought smaller companies and closed their factories to save on costs.

Cigarettes were suited to fast-paced city life. They were ideal for people who didn't have a lot of leisure time for smoking. Smoking was also a social activity. Offering a friend or stranger a smoke, lighting up together, sharing cigarette cards, or lending a match all became social rituals.

4 THE TOBACCO TRUST

James Duke built W. Duke, Sons & Co. into the nation's biggest tobacco company. In the late 1800s, it was easy to start a tobacco company. No federal patents protected cigarettes, and costs were fairly low. Any company could buy cured leaf and set up a factory to produce tobacco in any form. It simply needed the raw material, workers or machines to roll the product, and distribution outlets through which to sell it.

Thousands of small tobacco companies were doing business in the United States. Duke saw this as an opportunity to grow his company through diversification. With profits flowing into W. Duke, Sons & Co., he was able to purchase dozens of his competitors.

Duke also was looking for ways to improve his operations, including reducing advertising costs. He decided the best way to accomplish this was to merge with four major tobacco competitors. So in January 1890, the five companies formed the American Tobacco Company, which also became known as the "tobacco trust."[1] Duke named himself president of this new trust.

Poor families at the turn of the 1900s rolled cigarettes for small tobacco companies.

American Tobacco also purchased businesses that produced what it needed for manufacturing. These supplies included foil for the packages, licorice paste for flavorings, and small boxes for cigarettes and cigars. This allowed the company to manufacture its own packaging.

BRANDING

American Tobacco continued to create new brands and develop new images to sell those brands. Branding was a way to develop customer loyalty, generate repeat sales, and drive good word of mouth about tobacco products. Popular American Tobacco brands included Duke of Durham, Cameo, Cross Cut, and Duke's Best. Each brand had a distinctive package, with a design—including typeface and images—that quickly grew familiar to customers.

Before Duke created this brand loyalty among cigarette smokers, many people had simply bought tobacco in bulk. They purchased it by the pound

Tobacco and the Portable Flame

The rise of tobacco smoking brought with it the need to quickly light cigars, pipes, and cigarettes. At first, candles or sticks lit from open fires served this purpose. In 1830, French chemist Charles Sauria invented a self-igniting match using white phosphorous, a poisonous chemical. Then Gustaf Pasch of Sweden devised the safety match, a small stick of flammable material lit by striking it against a paper coated with red phosphorous. In 1889, Joshua Pusey, a prominent Pennsylvania attorney, invented book matches. He patented his design in 1892 and sold it to the Diamond Match Company, which became the first large-scale producer and distributor of matchbooks. Matchbooks were decorated with images and messages, making them popular collectibles.

from the barrels or jars in which shops displayed it. General stores were a common outlet for plug and pipe tobacco as well as cigars.

Social Smoking

Sharing, lending, and borrowing cigarettes made it easier for smokers to start conversations and make connections with people who share their habit. In the workplace, it is common for smokers to take their breaks together. The same happens at bars and restaurants, where smokers gather in designated outdoor areas to smoke and chat. When in need, smokers have also developed clever ways to get cigarettes. The writer George Orwell, famous for his books *1984* and *Animal Farm*, was once so poor he couldn't afford a pack of cigarettes. When going out, he would always bring a pack that held a single cigarette. He offered the cigarette to anyone he encountered. Strangers would refuse to take his last cigarette and then offer him one of their own.

In 1901, American Tobacco purchased a chain of retail stores, United Cigar Stores, from George J. Whelan. By selling directly through these stores, the company cut out middlemen and wholesalers, saving on costs. By 1910, there were more than 1,000 United Cigar stores throughout the country, with 300 in New York City alone.[2]

United Cigar shops had a standard layout and display for their merchandise. One store looked much like all the others, creating brand consistency and appeal for customers. American Tobacco also used the shops as a strategic business weapon to combat rival tobacco brands. When a local cigar store offered competing products, United would open up an outlet in the vicinity and temporarily slash its prices. This caused the rival stores to either stop offering competing brands or close up shop.

Cigar shops in the first decades of the 1900s featured displays designed to entice buyers.

SIDE EFFECTS

The American Tobacco Company took all the measures Duke could think of to save on costs. It closed down small factories, moving operations to larger plants in Richmond and New York. This saved on transportation costs and the expense of keeping the smaller factories open. However, American Tobacco kept the individual brand names it purchased. In this way, branded products remained available to loyal customers.

By 1902, American Tobacco was making more than 100 brands of cigarettes. The company controlled 60 percent of the tobacco market that was smoked or chewed.[3] James Duke also beat the competition through an agreement to use only Bonsack cigarette machines. In return, Bonsack agreed to charge American Tobacco a lower rate for the mechanized rolling machines than its competitors.

American Tobacco's success was not good for everybody. Duke hired only nonunion workers and paid them less than unionized employees. He drove hard bargains with tobacco growers, driving the price down to a few cents per pound. Since American Tobacco was their main and often only customer, most growers had little leverage to demand better prices. Duke's tobacco trust strived to control the market and prices for its products so that it could drive all competitors out of business.

BREAKING UP THE TOBACCO TRUST

American Tobacco's rivals claimed the company was competing unfairly. They claimed American Tobacco was driving up costs for consumers and purposefully trying to put its competitors out of business.

The federal government began paying attention. Other large companies, such as Standard Oil, were overpowering the free market by controlling the supply and the price of their goods. President Theodore Roosevelt, in office from 1901 to 1909, strongly favored antitrust laws such as the Sherman Antitrust Act of 1890. Passed under President Benjamin Harrison, the Sherman Antitrust Act prohibited anticompetitive business activities.

President Theodore Roosevelt also used the Sherman Antitrust Act to break up railroad monopolies.

Roosevelt believed American Tobacco and other powerful companies unfairly competed in the marketplace and forced consumers to pay artificially higher prices for their goods. Trusts such as these posed a danger to free enterprise, in Roosevelt's opinion, and he supported government actions to break them up.

In 1907, the federal government charged the tobacco company with violations of the Sherman Antitrust Act. The case went to the US Supreme Court, the highest court in the land. American

Antitrust Breakup Reconsidered

Not all historians agree the government should have broken up the American Tobacco trust. They point out that unlike Standard Oil, American Tobacco did not try to control the market through its raw material, tobacco. The company had not bought smaller companies against their will. The smaller companies had sold their brands and operations at prices considered fair. Some historians have also argued American Tobacco's actions made good business sense. Instead of being divided among thousands of producers, the tobacco market was consolidated into a smaller number of profitable companies. With American Tobacco's big distribution network, consumers had access to a greater range of brands than they had before at similar prices.

Tobacco argued it wasn't harming consumers. Instead, it said it had kept the price of tobacco low and had created a wide variety of products from which smokers could choose.

The case dragged on for four years as other antitrust actions worked their way through the courts. On May 15, 1911, the Supreme Court ruled against American Tobacco. By the court's order, the trust was broken up into four independent companies: American Tobacco, Liggett & Myers, Lorillard, and R. J. Reynolds.

After this decision, James Duke retired from American Tobacco. His years in the tobacco and cigarette business had made him a wealthy man. He turned to a new business interest, the electric power industry, founding Duke Energy. He also made generous donations to charities. One of the largest went to Trinity College in Durham, North Carolina. The college was later renamed Duke University in his family's honor.

At its manufacturing facilities, Liggett produces more than 120 distinct varieties of cigarettes.

LIGGETT & MYERS CO.

George S. Myers and John Edmund Liggett created Liggett & Myers Co. in 1873. American Tobacco acquired the company in 1899, but Liggett became independent again when the US Supreme Court declared American Tobacco was guilty of trust violations. Its first cigarette brand, L&M, was positioned as an upscale and exotic cigarette, using images of a veiled woman on its label.

In 1997, Liggett was the first company to offer a settlement to 22 states, acknowledging that tobacco caused health problems, including cancer. The settlement also admitted tobacco was addictive and was inappropriately marketed to teens. That did not sit well with other tobacco companies, which felt they would be forced to follow the example.

After the settlement, Liggett reduced its advertising efforts and concentrated on generic brands. It sold a number of its brands to the Philip Morris company. In 2001, after a disappointing launch of a brand called Jade, the company reorganized as Liggett Vector Brands.

GUARDS
CAMBRIDGE
MARLBORO
DERBY
ASCOT

THE 'SERPENT CIGARETTE'

5 | TOBACCO IMAGES

By the time James Duke founded American Tobacco, cigarette smoking had a reputation for being unhealthy. It was known to be an addictive habit, and some people claimed it was dangerous to health. Reverend George Trask, an antismoking crusader, founded the Anti-Tobacco Society in 1850. In his *Anti-Tobacco Journal*, Trask claimed,

> *I was a victim of tobacco—a tremulous, haggard clergyman, on the verge of the grave. I relinquished the poison; God smiled upon me, and I have been a robust and active man ever since; all who know me can testify. Believing then, as I now do, that Tobacco is as great a curse as can be named, I gave myself to battling it without compromise.*[1]

Trask believed cigarettes caused a wide range of health problems, including cancer. In his day, there were no scientific studies to support this belief. Still, many people believed nicotine was a poison. As a result, cigarette companies began worrying about the reputation of their product.

An 1880s cartoon depicts tobacco addiction as a snake made of cigarettes.

During the 1860s, Lorillard began offering Yacht Club pipe tobacco with the nicotine extracted. Advertisements for the product claimed this made these cigarettes healthy for smokers. Dr. Scott's Electric Cigarettes also appeared in the 1880s. This cigarette featured a small cotton filter that was supposed to protect the smoker from harmful chemicals. Filtered cigarettes then began appearing across the country.

Many saw tobacco as a corrupting influence on America's youth. They felt cigarettes led to alcohol abuse and a life of crime. New Jersey and Washington became the first states to ban the sale of tobacco to minors in 1883. The antitobacco movement gained strength alongside the temperance movement, which campaigned against the sale and consumption of alcoholic beverages. The leading antismoking crusader, Lucy Gaston, started out as a member of the Women's Christian Temperance Union. In 1890, Gaston founded the Anti-Cigarette League in Chicago.

Gaston won a wide following. The inventor Thomas Edison and the automaker Henry Ford joined the movement, promising not to hire cigarette smokers. But among the young, cigarettes still held the allure of glamour and worldliness as shown in magazine advertisements. Alice Roosevelt, daughter of President Theodore Roosevelt, shocked people by smoking in public. Many young women followed her example.

Not everybody believed tobacco smoking was harmful. Millions of people continued smoking and enjoying their habit. To one disapproving critic of smoking, Mark Twain wrote this stinging retort:

I don't want any of your statistics; I took your whole batch and lit my pipe with it. . . . I hate your kind of people. You are always ciphering out how much a man's health is injured, and how much his intellect is impaired, and how many pitiful dollars and cents he wastes in the course of ninety-two years' indulgence in the fatal practice of smoking. . . . I haven't a particle of confidence in a man who has no redeeming petty vices.[2]

Nevertheless, the tobacco prohibition movement gained strength. Between 1895 and 1921, 14 states banned cigarettes. But one by one, these states reversed their decisions. They needed money, and tobacco was a good source of tax income. Soon after repealing the bans on cigarettes, states added taxes on cigarettes to raise revenue.

SMOKING SOLDIERS

When World War I (1914–1918) erupted in Western Europe, cigarettes were popular on the front

President Grant: Smoker and Drinker

Ulysses S. Grant was a heavy drinker with a failing military career, but after winning key battles in the American Civil War, he won President Abraham Lincoln's confidence. He became a key leader of the US Army, and after the war, he was elected president. He continued drinking, but the real danger to Grant came from a heavy cigar habit. Grant smoked up to 20 cigars a day, and on July 23, 1885, soon after leaving office, he died of throat cancer.[3] He was one of the first public figures known to die of a smoking-related illness.

Many soldiers on both sides picked up a cigarette habit during World War I.

lines in France. British and German soldiers received regular rations of cigarettes. The United States entered the war in 1917. This gave cigarette companies a golden opportunity to market and promote their brands to US troops.

Cigarettes, mostly Camels, were donated and sold to US soldiers in Europe. Military and soldiers' aid organizations promoted smoking as a way to relieve the stress of combat. Smoking became a favored leisure activity for the troops, a welcome distraction from the war's hardships.

MARKETING TO WOMEN

After the war, cigarettes gained even more widespread public acceptance, boosted by print advertisements that associated smoking with glamour and achievement. Advertisers targeted women specifically. Newspaper and magazine ads suggested smoking enhanced attractiveness and worldliness.

Camels

After the Supreme Court broke up the American Tobacco trust, R. J. Reynolds set out to create a new national cigarette brand. In 1913, the company advertised camel parades to announce the new brand in small towns and big cities. Newspaper readers studied the company's strange new print advertisements and guessed at the meaning of "The Camels are Coming!"[4]

Camels, which blended Turkish and American tobacco, drew on the fad for cigarettes from Egypt and the Ottoman Empire. The pack, displaying a camel standing against a backdrop of palm trees and pyramids, cost ten cents, a nickel less than the competition.[5] Reynolds created a cartoon version of a camel, called Joe Camel, in 1987. Children quickly began recognizing the image along with their favorite animated television characters.

Smoking by women was still controversial. Smoking was largely a male activity. Cigars were associated with business tycoons and politicians. Many looked on female smokers with unease. They felt a woman who smoked defied convention and risked a life of immorality. In an era when women were fighting for basic rights, including the right to vote, smoking became a symbol of independence and equality with men.

American Tobacco, makers of Lucky Strike cigarettes, targeted women with the slogan "Reach for a Lucky Instead of a Sweet."[6] The campaign first appeared in 1925 and was designed to appeal to diet- and weight-conscious women. Instead of eating fattening candy, the campaign implied, smokers should light up for the sake of their waistlines and their health. Advertisers began associating cigarette smoking with weight loss.

The campaign was successful, making Lucky Strike the best-selling cigarette brand for two years running. But candy companies strongly objected to it. Several companies threatened to sue American Tobacco for slandering their product. Critics also pointed out American Tobacco was using the ads to target younger smokers, who were key customers for the candy industry.

In 1920, women finally won the right to vote, giving women a sense of power and freedom. In 1929, women smoking Lucky Strikes marched in New York's Easter Sunday parade. Smoking was associated with the liberated woman. To develop the market, the Philip Morris tobacco company organized smoking classes for women, conducted by Florence Linden, a registered nurse. Linden

A 1939 advertisement still made use of Lucky Strike's successful slogan.

taught proper smoking etiquette, concentrating on common bad habits of both sexes. She cautioned that women shouldn't puff like a steam engine, and men shouldn't douse a cigarette under the kitchen faucet.

Philip Morris later introduced Virginia Slims with the slogan "You've Come a Long Way, Baby."[7] The slimmer cigarette was supposed to appeal to notions of fashion and personal style. It made a statement: cigarette-smoking women could be liberated and glamorous at the same time. For some women, smoking represented freedom from old taboos.

Cigarettes on Stage

Whether women ought to smoke was a hot topic of debate in the late 1800s. The controversy reached the stage, where playwrights and composers often took up social issues. The musical *Runaway Girl* featured a daring young woman who sang "Sly Cigarette" while smoking on stage:

> *If girls and boys*
> *Were asked what joys*
> *They found the most entrancing.*
> *Each boy would name*
> *His fav'rite game*
> *From "Ducks and Drakes" to dancing.*

> *But girls with me*
> *Would all agree,*
> *Although you think I'm joking.*
> *With twinkling eye,*
> *They'd make reply*
> *"The best of all is smoking." Ah!*

> *Oh, sly cigarette!*
> *Oh, fie cigarette!*
> *Why did you teach me to love you so,*
> *When I have to pretend that I don't,*
> *you know?*[8]

CIGARETTE
TAXES

Tobacco has long been a key source of tax income for the federal government. In the 1920s, the states began collecting tobacco taxes as well, starting with Iowa in 1921. By 1950, 40 states and the District of Columbia had cigarette taxes. The taxes ranged from one cent to 21 cents per pack. Cities and counties also taxed cigarettes. In 1969, North Carolina became the fiftieth state to impose a cigarette tax. By 2014, combined local taxes on a pack of cigarettes in Chicago, Illinois, reached $6.16.[9]

$0.00–
$0.99

$1.00–
$1.99

$2.00–
$2.99

$3.00–
$3.99

$4.00+

AK
$2.00

HI
$3.20

Cigarette Taxes per Pack, 2014

WA $3.03

OR $1.18

MT $1.70

ND $0.44

MN $2.83

ME $2.00

ID $0.57

WY $0.60

SD $1.53

WI $2.52

MI $2.00

NY $4.35

NV $0.80

UT $1.70

CO $0.84

NE $0.64

IA $1.36

PA $1.60

CA $0.87

KS $0.79

MO $0.17

IL $1.98

IN $1.00

OH $1.25

WV $0.55

VA $0.30

AZ $2.00

NM $1.66

OK $1.03

AR $1.15

KY $0.60

NC $0.45

TN $0.62

SC $0.57

TX $1.41

MS $0.68

AL $0.43

GA $0.37

LA $0.36

FL $1.34

VT $2.62

NH $1.78

MA $3.51

RI $3.50

CT $3.40

NJ $2.70

DE $1.60

MD $2.00

DC $2.68

CANADA

MEXICO

PACIFIC OCEAN

GULF OF MEXICO

ATLANTIC OCEAN

6 | THE CIGARETTE AGE

Although cigarette smoking was widely popular by the middle of the 1900s, cigarette companies had a problem. The public was growing worried about the health effects of smoking. People saw the harmful effects went beyond scratchy throats and coughing. Many scientists were studying lung cancer, a dangerous and often fatal disease. During the 1920s, the number of lung cancer cases began to rise. The increase continued through the 1930s and 1940s.

Lung cancer was a rare disease, and tobacco companies pointed out that the rise in lung cancer cases could have different causes. Starting in the 1920s, for example, states and cities were paving dirt roads—perhaps asphalt dust kicked up by the paving process, they suggested, could be causing health problems. Cancer among the soldiers returning from France after World War I could be a result of poison gas used on the battlefields. Many pointed to the global influenza epidemic that began in 1918 as a possible culprit. Perhaps the poisonous smoke churned out by factories producing steel, cars, and other industrial goods was to blame.

By midcentury, smoking was widely popular despite its suspected health risks.

HEALTHY CIGARETTES?

Cigarette companies used advertising to respond to the health worries. American Tobacco created a new slogan for Lucky Strike cigarettes, claiming "It's toasted." The toasting process was supposed to get rid of the irritating chemicals in cigarette smoke. This, it was claimed, made Lucky Strike tobacco easier on the throat and lungs. To emphasize the point, new print ads showed doctors enjoying Lucky Strikes. One ad from 1930 claimed, "20,679 Physicians Say Luckies are Less Irritating."[1]

Filtered cigarettes were also designed to calm fears. In 1924, Philip Morris created a new filtered brand for women. The ad campaign for the new product, Marlboros, claimed these new cigarettes were "Mild as May."[2] Their filters had a red stripe intended to hide lipstick stains. Later in the 1900s, the company began marketing Marlboros to men, using the image of a cowboy known as the Marlboro man. At least four of the men who portrayed the Marlboro man died of smoking-related diseases, the last one in 2014.

Tar and Nicotine

Scientific research has proven nicotine is highly addictive. It also has determined cigarettes, cigars, chewing tobacco, and other forms of tobacco cause cancer. But nicotine itself is not carcinogenic. It is the tobacco smoke that contains carcinogenic chemicals. There are more than 7,000 chemicals in tobacco smoke, including carbon monoxide and tar.[3] Carbon monoxide is poisonous to the lungs. *Tar* describes the compounds that stay in the lungs after smoking. Because they stick to the body's throat and lungs, the compounds reminded researchers of the sticky road asphalt.

The rough-and-ready Marlboro man portrays an image of extreme manliness.

NEW RESEARCH ON SMOKING

Medical investigators in the United Kingdom and the United States began looking into the startling rise in deaths from lung cancer. The results showed a strong correlation between the increase in cigarette smoking since World War I and the deadly disease. In the 1930s, scientists began carrying out population studies. Their goal was to discover the link between lung cancer and smoking by using statistics. They compared groups of lung cancer patients to those who were cancer-free.

Many scientists and doctors believed using statistics was not enough. They demanded better medical evidence to connect cancer to smoking. In 1931, to delve deeper into the effects of tobacco, Angel Roffo of Argentina applied tobacco smoke to the skins of rabbits. Many of the rabbits developed tumors. Through the 1930s, Roffo carried out more experiments to confirm his suspicion that tobacco smoking was a direct cause of cancer. Franz-Hermann Müller carried out important statistical studies at Cologne Hospital in Germany in 1939. Subsequently, more studies were carried out in different countries. The researchers found in general that a higher percentage of the patients with lung cancer were smokers.

The 1950s was a productive decade for tobacco research. In 1953, three scientists set out to find conclusive evidence linking tobacco and cancer. In a famous study, Ernst Wynder, Evarts Graham, and Adele Croninger used lab mice. They painted a substance distilled from cigarette smoke on the skin of the mice. A high percentage of the mice developed cancerous tumors.

In public, tobacco companies claimed these studies did not prove the link between cancer and smoking. Privately, they conducted their own research and came to the same conclusion: there was indeed a link between cigarette smoking and cancer. Despite the bad news, one executive saw an opportunity for his own company, writing "Boy! Wouldn't it be wonderful if our company was first

New and Improved?

The Lorillard Tobacco Company responded to the bad news about smokers and health by developing a micronite filter for its Kent cigarettes. The company claimed this was "a pure, dust-free, completely harmless material that is so safe, so effective, it actually is used to help filter the air in operating rooms of leading hospitals."[6]

Lorillard ran ads in medical journals and sent gifts of Kent cigarettes to doctors, explaining that Kent's represented a new and healthy option for smokers. Unfortunately, the new micronite filter had problems. It was made of cotton, crepe paper, acetate, and asbestos. Although asbestos makes good filter material, it is also extremely carcinogenic. Employees at the plant who made the Kent filters died at a high rate from lung cancer and asbestos-related illnesses. Kent smokers may also have been affected. After 16 months, the company stopped the use of micronite.

to produce a cancer-free cigarette. What we could do to the competition!"[4]

FIGHTING BACK

The tobacco industry fought back against the emerging scientific consensus that cigarettes were harmful. Six of the cigarette industry's leaders met in December 1953 to come up with a strategy. They agreed to hire Hill and Knowlton, a public relations firm, to help them make the case for cigarettes. Hill and Knowlton's job was to give the tobacco industry's side of the argument. A company memo described an important part of the campaign:

We should create a committee with "research" in the title so that the public recognizes the existence of weighty scientific views which hold there is no proof that cigarette smoking is a cause of lung cancer.[5]

This led cigarette manufacturers to create the Tobacco Industry Research Committee (TIRC) in

January 1954. The TIRC gave the impression it was doing serious scientific research into smoking and tobacco. It would pose challenges to lab research showing cigarettes caused harm. It asked these questions: Why did more men than women get lung cancer, even though women were taking up smoking at a faster rate than men? What was the genetic basis for cancer? Why did nonsmokers also suffer from cancer and heart disease? Why did some famous men and women smoke well into their old age with no health effects?

The plan of the cigarette companies was to create doubt about cancer and other health research. They would do this by exploiting any controversy, explaining that many scientists were still skeptical of smoking's link to cancer. Unfortunately for the TIRC and the tobacco industry, research into cigarettes continued, as did the rise in lung cancer. With the results of medical studies appearing regularly in the press, the public began understanding and believing the connection.

GLAMOROUS SMOKING

In an effort to maintain the glamorous image of their products, tobacco companies turned to actors to directly promote cigarettes in movies. When moviegoers saw their favorite stars lighting up on the big screen, they got the message that smoking gave people star quality. This practice went back to the days of early cigarette cards, which featured star baseball players and other athletes.

In 1932, the White Owl cigar company made an agreement with the movie studio Warner Brothers. White Owl paid $250,000 for the right to claim actor Paul Muni smoked its products in the

Smoking in movies such as Breakfast at Tiffany's, starring Audrey Hepburn, promoted cigarettes to viewers.

gangster movie *Scarface.*[7] In 1935, cigarette-maker Brown and Williamson produced a short cartoon to be shown before or after a movie. The cartoon showed a flight of penguins dropping cartons of Kool cigarettes over New York City, and it featured the Statue of Liberty blowing smoke rings from Kool cigarettes. A 1950 print ad for Chesterfield cigarettes depicted actor and future president

Ronald Reagan claiming, "I'm sending Chesterfields to all my friends. That's the merriest Christmas any smoker can have—Chesterfield mildness plus no unpleasant after-taste."[8] The ad showed Reagan sitting at a desk autographing Chesterfield cartons, which were colorfully decorated with a Christmas scene.

But using the images of famous smokers, once an effective way to promote cigarettes, began backfiring as the stars suffered the health consequences. Humphrey Bogart, a well-known movie actor, was often seen in films in smoke-filled rooms holding a cigarette. For millions of people, Bogart made smoking cool. He died of throat cancer in 1957. Other well-known entertainers would eventually die from smoking-related illnesses. These included Louis Armstrong, Johnny Carson, Nat King Cole, Gary Cooper, Sammy Davis Jr., Walt Disney, Duke Ellington, George Harrison, Steve McQueen, and Jesse Owens.

Fred, Barney, and Winstons

At one time, it was common practice for cigarette companies to sponsor television shows and sporting events. The *Flintstones*, a popular animated prime-time show that aired in the 1960s, was sponsored by Winston cigarettes. Two of the show's Stone Age characters, Fred Flintstone and Barney Rubble, even appeared in commercials smoking Winstons. But in 1970, Congress passed an act banning cigarette ads on television and radio. In 1986, the Flintstones did a public service announcement for the American Cancer Association.

7 | TOBACCO IN COURT

After years of medical research, tobacco companies still denied the link between cigarettes and cancer. Instead, the companies claimed the researchers had doubts about their findings. Cancer had many different causes. Smoking might be a little risky, perhaps, but many activities were a little risky. Driving, walking in the rain, and even taking a bath could be risky. Why, companies asked, should a smoker give up smoking, since there were so many other everyday risks?

Nevertheless, smokers who suffered from cancer and other ailments began suing tobacco companies in the 1950s. They claimed cigarettes had harmed them and forced them to spend money on doctors and hospitals for smoking-related illnesses. For many years, the companies successfully defended these cases. They argued there was no proven link between cancer and smoking. They made it a policy not to settle a case or admit liability for smoking-related illnesses.

The US government stepped into the debate in 1964. That year, the surgeon general released "Smoking and Health: Report of the Advisory Committee to the Surgeon General of the Public Health Service." The surgeon general is the leading spokesperson and

Ads promoted cigarettes as doctors' favorite brands or discussed supposed health benefits.

policy maker for health in the United States. This report was the first government research document linking smoking to lung cancer and heart disease. Many doctors praised the long and detailed report. At the same time, it raised opposition from tobacco companies. President Lyndon Johnson was facing a reelection campaign in the same year. Not wanting to lose votes in the southern tobacco states, he refused to endorse the report.

Regardless, the report triggered changes in US law. A 1965 law required tobacco companies to print a health warning on each pack of cigarettes. The US government has developed new warnings over the years. By 2009, nine different statements appeared on cigarette packs, including:

Cigarettes cause fatal lung cancer

Smoking during pregnancy can harm your baby

Quitting smoking now greatly reduces serious risks to your health

Smoking can kill you[1]

THE *CIPOLLONE* CASE

In the meantime, lawsuits against tobacco companies continued to be unsuccessful. A breakthrough occurred in the case of *Cipollone v. Liggett*. This case was brought by the family of Rose Cipollone, a New Jersey housewife. Cipollone began smoking Chesterfields, made by Liggett, at age 16. Worried about her health, she switched to L&M, which had a filter and which Liggett

SURGEON GENERAL'S WARNING:
Smoking Causes Lung Cancer,
Heart Disease, Emphysema, And
May Complicate Pregnancy.

promoted as "just what the doctor ordered."[2] She smoked a pack and a half of cigarettes a day, every day, until she came down with lung cancer in her fifties. In 1983, she sued Philip Morris, Lorillard, and Liggett. The suit claimed the cigarette makers did not warn her cigarettes were addictive and a serious danger to health.

The case dragged on for years. Rose Cipollone died in 1984, but her family carried on the lawsuit. The court finally ruled Liggett would have to pay $400,000 to Cipollone's family.[3] Because Liggett's advertising implied its cigarettes were healthier, it was liable for Cipollone's death. Philip Morris and Lorillard escaped the decision, as Cipollone had started smoking their brands after cigarette warnings appeared in 1966.

Liggett appealed the decision and won. Cipollone's family then appealed to the US Supreme Court. While the Cipollones eventually dropped the case, their efforts paved the way for future lawsuits. On June 24, 1992, the court said individuals can sue tobacco companies for any false statements. They could also bring tobacco companies to court for misleading people about the dangers of smoking.

THE WHISTLE-BLOWER

Tobacco companies have large budgets for research. They hire scientists to examine the chemical properties of tobacco smoke, develop new cigarette flavors, and test the effects of smoking on the body. They are not required, however, to make their findings public, and they require employees to sign confidentiality agreements. In these contracts, employees promise to keep the research and test results a secret and never discuss their findings with the press.

Jeffrey Wigand worked as a research scientist for Brown and Williamson, makers of Viceroy and other brands. He eventually became a vice president of research and development. In March 1993, after bitter disagreements with other executives, he was fired.

Wigand was neither proud of the work he carried out at Brown and Williamson nor happy with the company's treatment of him and other employees. In 1995, Wigand agreed to be a witness for the state of Mississippi against the tobacco companies. He testified tobacco companies knew nicotine was highly addictive. Moreover, he testified the companies had purposely raised the nicotine content to make them even more addictive. The *Wall Street Journal* ran a front-page story giving the testimony in detail.

In 1996, Wigand appeared on the popular television news show *60 Minutes*. During this interview, he claimed Brown and Williamson knew cigarettes were addictive and harmful. The company also knew certain chemicals added to the cigarettes caused cancer. However, the company had kept its findings secret.

The Healthy Cigarette

Scientists at Liggett & Myers worked through the 1960s and 1970s to develop a "safe" cigarette. If successful, this product would not cause cancer in laboratory mice or in humans. By 1978, the XA Project, as it was called, was almost ready for release. But the company finally decided against the new cigarette. In the company's view, selling the new product would be admitting its traditional cigarettes were dangerous to health.

Mississippi won the case, after which the tobacco companies agreed to pay a $246 billion settlement.[4] As a whistle-blower, however, Wigand had broken his confidentiality agreement. He received threats over the phone. Thieves broke into his home to steal documents. Fearing violence, he went into hiding and hired a 24-hour bodyguard.

MORE LAWSUITS

The *Cipollone* case and Wigand's testimony opened a busy era of lawsuits against tobacco companies. Individual states claimed the companies were responsible for public health costs for smoking-related illnesses. The tobacco companies responded that smokers were responsible for their own health. After all, cigarette packs carried a health warning, so anyone who bought one must know the dangers.

The legal battle turned around when documents leaked by insiders showed tobacco companies had run secret studies of their own. As a result of this in-house research, it was clear the companies knew the dangers of nicotine addiction. In February 2000, a jury in California awarded a smoker $51.5 million in damages from Philip Morris.[5] Lawsuits are expensive for both sides, no matter who wins. Instead of continuing to fight in court, the tobacco companies and the states called a truce in November 1998. Tobacco companies agreed to a Master Settlement Agreement. This would settle the cases with the states.

According to the agreement, tobacco companies would stop marketing to minors. They would pay the states for their health costs, $10 billion a year for 25 years.[6] They would also pay for the

Wigand cried at a news conference when the tobacco company settlement was announced.

National Public Education Foundation. This group would help educate people, especially children, about the dangers of cigarette smoking.

Although the tobacco industry settled with the states, individuals continued bringing cases against them. By 2015, Philip Morris and R. J. Reynolds were receiving court decisions in the $300 million range. One case for wrongful death in Florida brought an award of $23.6 billion to

Truth Ads

By the Master Settlement Agreement, tobacco companies agreed to fund antismoking advertising campaigns. In 1998, the money helped to start the American Legacy Foundation. This group created the Truth campaign, which appeared in print ads and on television. The goal of the campaign was to reduce smoking among teenagers. By 2015, the rate of smoking among high school students had fallen to approximately 15 percent, the lowest in 22 years.[9]

But the Truth campaign ran into trouble when its ads targeted Philip Morris by using the company's name. One ad showed a young person walking into the company's offices with a briefcase marked "lie detector." Showing specific company names was a violation of the Master Settlement Agreement, and the group pulled the ads in response.

the widow of a smoker. But on appeal, the award was reduced to $17 million.[7]

Tobacco companies also had to defend class-action lawsuits, in which a large group of people join together to sue one or more defendants. Each person in the class must prove addiction to cigarettes caused him or her harm. If the court and the jury agree, then they set an award each member of the class shares. In a single case, *Engle v. Liggett*, a court awarded $145 billion in damages to more than 700,000 class members.[8] Tobacco companies defend these lawsuits at great cost in legal fees. They often claim a cause of a person's death is uncertain and cigarettes are not necessarily to blame. They also argue adults know the risks of smoking.

Children in New York rally against smoking as part of Kick Butts Day, a national day for antismoking activism organized by the nonprofit Campaign for Tobacco-Free Kids.

THE MORE
TOBACCO ADS I SEE,
THE MORE LIKELY I AM
TO START SMOKING.
Mount Sinai
The Partnership
NYC COALITION FOR A SMOKE-FREE CITY
MANHATTAN SMOKE-FREE PARTNERSHIP

8 | THE TOBACCO BUSINESS

Tobacco remains a big business in the United States. Producers made 56.2 million small cigars, 4.4 billion cigars, 2.3 million pounds (1 million kg) of pipe tobacco, and 24.5 billion cigarettes in the month of April 2016.[1]

For all of the changes in the industry, however, tobacco growing hasn't changed much in 300 years. Plants still begin as seedlings in a seedbed where they are protected, usually by linen coverings. When the seedlings are mature they are transplanted into the main field by hand or by a machine called a transplanter. Topping is still used to help the plant grow. Farmers harvest their crops by cutting the leaves off the plants, either before or after they mature. Curing is an essential part of the process. To carry this out, growers gradually raise the temperature in the barn or warehouse. Once the leaves are dry and yellow, a little humidity is reintroduced so the leaves can be handled without crumbling. The leaves, along with the stems, are then processed into a pulp. To mask the bitter smoke created by the stems, growers may add sugar to the mixture. For many smokers, sugar also makes cigarettes more addictive.

In the past, cigarettes were sold in machines. Today, cigarette machines are found in the United States only in places that restrict entry to people under 18.

Growers sort tobacco leaves according to their color, size, and quality. Each tobacco company has employees who inspect and grade the tobacco that comes from the growers. At one time, company representatives and growers took part in auctions at tobacco warehouses. During and after the harvest season, these auctions were an occasion for growers to meet and talk business, as well as sell their crop to the highest bidder. While there are still a few auctions, most tobacco companies now find it more efficient to set the price through contracts with individual growers. This eliminates the need for auctions and big tobacco warehouses.

The definition of each grade of tobacco is precise. The US Department of Agriculture has developed a long list of official descriptions. For example, one category is known as M4FFair Quality Mixed Groups. This tobacco shows "ripe, firm leaf structure, heavy, lean in oil. Injury tolerance 30 percent, of which not over 10 percent may be waste."[2]

At the factory, tobacco leaf is loaded into a hopper. A paper roll is placed on a conveyor belt.

Unique Perique

At one time, tobacco companies bought their cured leaves at auction from independent growers. In the 2000s, most growers work under contract and send their crop to a single company. As independent contractors, they know they'll get the contracted price for their crop. A few independent growers remain, including Ray Martin. On his small farm in Saint James Parish in Louisiana, Martin grows the pungent perique variety, selling it directly to a variety of tobacco companies. Similar to wine, his tobacco goes through fermentation in oak barrels. After a year, it comes out of the barrel. Before it goes into a cigarette, perique is blended with other, milder tobaccos because smoking pure perique leaf makes most people ill.

The machinery inserts tobacco into the paper, then forms and glues the paper into a long, thin tube. The tube is then cut into the right lengths for cigarettes. Finally, the machine inserts a filter onto the end of the cigarette.

SELLING TOBACCO

Tobacco companies sell most of their products through tobacco and convenience stores. The number of cigarettes sold changes each year, and cigarette brands rise and fall in popularity. Taxes on cigarettes have been going up. Combined federal, state, and local taxes added up to $20.92 per carton of ten packs in 2014 and $21.32 per carton in 2016. New York levies a state tax of $4.35 per pack, the highest in the nation.[3] These taxes and other similar taxes are favored by lawmakers as an easy way to raise money. Others hope making cigarettes more expensive will encourage people to quit smoking.

But there is a financial argument against high taxes on cigarettes. Federal, state, and local governments tax cigarettes at a higher rate than other consumer items. These taxes are regressive, meaning they generally hit lower-income people the hardest. High taxes can also lead to black market and illegal cross-border trade.

Kip Viscusi, a professor at Vanderbilt University, argues tobacco taxes are too high. One reason is because they bring in more money than states actually spend on medical care for smoking-related diseases:

To be sure, smokers do incur higher medical costs—about five cents per pack in Massachusetts in the mid-1990s. Yet, because smokers have a shorter life expectancy than nonsmokers, smokers incur a cost of 11 cents per pack less in nursing home costs and 9 cents per pack less in pension costs. On balance, smokers incur about 14 cents less per pack in costs paid by Massachusetts, while contributing an additional 51 cents per pack in excise taxes.[4]

Nevertheless, tobacco taxes are considered as essential to funding public services as other taxes such as income taxes, business taxes, license fees, and road tolls. By 2016, the federal tax rate had reached an all-time high of $1.01 a pack.[5]

Tobacco is still a profitable business for the largest multinational producer, Philip Morris. This company employs 82,000 people and in 2014 held 15.5 percent of the global market outside the United States. Philip Morris makes Marlboro, the world's most popular brand, and is active in 180 national markets.[6]

Mergers and acquisitions have led to dominance of the international market by four big companies: Philip Morris, British American Tobacco, Japan Tobacco, and Imperial Tobacco. Many foreign countries have a country-wide monopoly on cigarette manufacturing in their own countries.

The Black Market State

New York State levies the highest cigarette tax in the nation. It is also the home of a big tobacco black market. By some estimates, nearly two-thirds of all cigarettes sold in New York are smuggled in from other states.[7] Producers disguise the packs with fake tax stamps, which are supposed to prove that they've paid the New York rate.

A worker inspects tobacco in a German cigarette factory owned by Philip Morris International.

PHILIP MORRIS

Philip Morris International is the largest tobacco company in the United States. The business was established by an English tobacco seller who opened his first shop in London's Bond Street in 1847. The company eventually made its headquarters in Richmond, Virginia.

A single brand, Marlboro, vaulted Philip Morris to the top of the US tobacco industry. By 2016, Marlboro was the leading brand in all 50 US states and held 44 percent of the retail market. This share is greater than the following ten brands combined.[8]

In 2003, the original Philip Morris Company rebranded itself as the Altria Group. By changing its name, the company sought to improve its image. *Altria* would remind consumers the company made more than cigarettes. At the time, Altria owned Kraft Foods, which makes Velveeta, Kool-Aid, Jell-O, and other famous grocery brands. In 2007, Altria spun off Kraft to Altria shareholders. In a spinoff, a parent company surrenders control of a smaller company. This allows the smaller company to operate independently.

The world's largest producer by volume is the China National Tobacco Corporation, which sold 2.3 trillion cigarettes in 2009.[9]

INCREASING REGULATIONS

Many foreign markets are placing new restrictions on tobacco sale and use. In some countries, these laws now extend to the cigarette pack. In 2012, Australia became the first country in the world to require plain packaging. This means cigarettes sold in the country must appear in a standardized package without brand colors or logos. The idea is to limit the appeal of smoking, especially to young people. Each pack also must carry a large health warning on the dangers of cigarette smoking. In the United Kingdom, similar plain packaging began in 2016.

Tobacco companies have been fighting plain packaging requirements. Philip Morris has filed a lawsuit against plain packaging in Australia. It also sued Uruguay after the South American country passed a law requiring health warnings to cover 80 percent of each cigarette pack.[10]

Tobacco companies have another legal tangle: restrictions on smoking in public places. Restrictions such as these date to 1575, when Mexico banned smoking in all of its churches. Modern scientific studies on secondhand smoke have given antismoking laws a further boost.

Secondhand smoke, or passive smoke, is what nonsmokers breathe when they are in the vicinity of smoke from a burning cigarette, cigar, pipe, or hookah being used to smoke tobacco. In 1986, the American government issued the surgeon general's report on secondhand smoke.

Ad campaigns seek to educate the public on the dangers of secondhand smoke.

Secondhand smoke kills.

The report described the dangers to people who didn't smoke but were subjected to secondhand smoke. Research showed cigarette smoke contained the same chemicals whether it was inhaled or floating in the air. Therefore, anyone who took in secondhand smoke was also exposed to carcinogenic chemicals.

Not all studies support this conclusion. Ange Wang, a medical student at Stanford University, studied the effects of active and passive smoking on 76,000 women.[11] She published her study in 2013. Although Wang found active smokers had a higher risk of lung cancer, she came to a different conclusion for those exposed only to secondhand smoke. She found no increased risk, unless the nonsmoker lived with a smoker for a long period of time.

Other studies have come to similar conclusions. But that has not discouraged US states and cities from passing antismoking laws to protect nonsmokers. In 1975, Minnesota passed the Clean Indoor Air Act, banning smoking in some public places. In 1977, Berkeley, California, passed the first law banning smoking in restaurants. Nearby San Francisco followed in 1983, restricting smoking in private offices and workplaces.

One of the largest groups of individuals claiming damage from secondhand smoke is flight attendants who flew during the years when smoking was allowed on airliners. A significant number of flight attendants developed lung and breathing problems, even though they weren't smokers. In 1991, seven flight attendants filed a lawsuit. Although they lost, on appeal a Florida court allowed the case to proceed as a class action suit. Over several years, more than 60,000 nonsmoking flight attendants joined *Broin et al vs. Philip Morris*. In a 1997 settlement, the court awarded more than $300 million to be used to create a foundation to study the effects of secondhand smoke.[12] The settlement would also cover legal fees and the fees of the attendants' attorneys. Though the suit did not award money directly to the flight attendants, it did clear the way for them to sue the tobacco companies individually. Some subsequent cases have awarded some flight attendants significant settlements.

There are smoking bans of one sort or another in all 50 states. But there's also opposition to the policy. Several groups are calling for an end to new smoking restrictions or a repeal of laws that already exist. They believe smokers have certain rights that antismoking laws violate. They also point out that banning cigarettes in restaurants violates the right of restaurant owners to decide whether to allow smoking.

Tobacco Up in the Air

Smoking bans came early to the aviation industry. In 1973, the Civil Aeronautics Board required all planes on commercial flights to have no-smoking sections. In 1988, the US Congress passed a total ban on smoking on all domestic (US-only) flights of two hours or less. In 1989, a new law banned smoking on all flights beginning and ending in the United States lasting six hours or less. That means that of 16,000 regularly scheduled flights a year, only 28 routes, mostly between Hawaii and the US mainland, allowed smoking.[13] In 1995, Delta became the first commercial airline with a no-smoking policy on all of its planes.

Copenhagen
SNUFF
Copenhagen®
SNUFF
FreshCope.com
NET WT. 1.2 OZ.
Tax Class M
U.S. SMOKELESS
TOBACCO
NASHVILLE, TN

9 | NEW MARKETS, NEW PRODUCTS

As tobacco smoking among US consumers has declined, the tobacco industry has had to adapt or see profits shrink. State and national governments place heavy restrictions on tobacco advertising. Taxes on cigarettes remain in place, some growing higher every year. Lawsuits by smokers against tobacco companies continue. Nevertheless, these businesses remain profitable. Reynolds American sold $10.6 billion worth of products in 2015 and earned a profit of $3.2 billion.[1]

As public companies, tobacco companies have millions of shareholders. Ordinary people from all walks of life, as well as pension funds, mutual funds, banks, and other investors, own shares. For these groups, the companies have an important duty. Executives do the best they can to make the company more profitable and the shares more valuable.

SMOKELESS AND SNUFF

To reach that goal, tobacco companies are selling a wider variety of products. In the 1800s, before cigarettes became widely popular, plug was the most popular kind of tobacco.

Tobacco companies sell a wide range of products, including multiple forms of smokeless tobacco, to keep profits up.

Users would tear off a plug or twist of cured leaf from a pouch or a can, put it in their mouth, and chew away. When they were done, they would spit the plug on the ground or into a spittoon. Using tobacco this way was cheaper than smoking cigars or pipes.

Smokeless tobacco is the modern version of plug tobacco. It goes in the mouth and is chewed and positioned between the teeth and the gums for a nicotine boost. To soften the grainy, bitter taste of ground tobacco, and to associate it with healthier food products, manufacturers add different flavors, including cinnamon, berry, and apple. Snuff is ground-up tobacco that can be chewed or sniffed. Snus is snuff that is packed into pouches that look like small tea bags. Smokeless tobacco also comes in the form of strips, lozenges, or sticks that dissolve in the mouth. No spitting is necessary.

The US Smokeless Tobacco Company, owned by Altria, manufactures dozens of brands of smokeless tobacco, including Skoal and Copenhagen. The Copenhagen brand is almost two centuries

Smoking Cubans

Cuba has long been famous as the home of the most popular cigars in the world. But in 1962, US President John F. Kennedy signed an embargo on trade between the United States and Cuba because of Cuba's ties with the Soviet Union, a US rival. Because of the embargo, no US company or person was allowed to buy or transport Cuban products to the United States.

Everything changed in 2016, when US president Barack Obama announced a new policy on trade with Cuba. Individual Americans could now bring $100 worth of Cuban cigars back to the United States. The Cuban cigar industry eagerly awaited the next step, an end to the embargo on commercial trade. Access to the vast market for cigars in the United States would likely give a boost to Cuban tobacco growers.

old and brings in more than $1 billion in sales every year.[2] Similar to cigarette companies, US Smokeless develops complex formulas the company keeps secret, which include tobacco but also water, salt, ethyl alcohol, sodium, ammonium carbonate, sodium saccharine, and various flavors and preservatives.

Reynolds American also competes in the smokeless market with Camel brands of snuff and snus. Reynolds has merged with subsidiary companies that make smokeless tobacco products. In 2006, it purchased the American Snuff Company of Memphis. By buying smaller companies, a large corporation increases its collection of brands, as well as its revenue stream.

E-CIGS AND VAPING

E-cigarettes have a small amount of nicotine, which is extracted from tobacco. Smokers who smoke regular cigarettes sometimes try e-cigs as a way of quitting the tobacco habit. Most e-cigarettes look like ordinary cigarettes, but they don't produce any flame or smoke. Using them is sometimes accepted in public places that ban smoking, or in offices and homes that do not allow cigarettes.

Instead of a match and a flame, e-cigs operate on a small, rechargeable battery. Inside the device is a cartridge that transforms liquid to vapor. Because of this, smoking e-cigarettes is called vaping. The liquid cartridges are made in different flavors.

Tobacco companies have paid attention to the e-cig trend. Lorillard, the oldest tobacco company in the United States, owns Blu, the e-cig brand with the largest market share. Lorillard

and other tobacco firms already have significant distribution networks for their products in the form of smoke shops, cigar stores, and convenience stores. They also have huge budgets devoted to marketing the new products.

Nevertheless, vaping may have its own dangers. Studies on users have shown chemicals in the vapor negatively affect cells that fight infection in the nose, throat, and lungs. Vaping is not allowed in many places, such as US domestic airlines, where a regular smoking ban is in effect.

NEW MARKETS ABROAD

In the early 2000s, the US market for cigarettes has seen little growth. In 2014, approximately 16.8 percent of adults in the United States smoked, compared to 42.4 percent in 1965.[3] States and cities frequently pass new restrictions on cigarette smoking in public places. Often laws require smokers to position themselves a certain distance from a business' entrance. Smoking is also banned in many private spaces, such as hotel rooms and apartments.

As smoking cigarettes has decreased in the United States, tobacco companies have spread their marketing overseas.

Marketing cigarettes in the United States is also a challenge. There are few advertising venues available. Tobacco companies can't advertise on television or billboards. Today, television viewers and moviegoers rarely see their favorite stars smoking a cigarette, unless the show or movie takes place in an era when smoking was allowed and popular.

Fake Cigarettes

Counterfeiting is a big industry in China, including counterfeit tobacco. The city of Yunxiao, in Fujian Province, is the heart of Chinese cigarette counterfeiting. Small, secret factories and workshops dot the town and the hillsides or hide tucked away underground, in caves, and behind locked doors. The cigarettes are made with dried leaves laced with tobacco, with printed packs that imitate the real thing. The market is huge—by one estimate, 400 billion fake Marlboros and other brands were produced in 2007 alone, making up one-third of the total market in China.[5]

To grow sales, tobacco companies are looking to foreign markets. Outside the United States and Europe, cigarette sales are still rising. An important reason is fewer restrictions in Asian, Middle Eastern, and African nations on tobacco products. By 2014, the Asian Pacific region, including China, made up 65 percent of the global cigarette market.[4]

Dominated by the China National Tobacco Corporation, the Chinese market is closed to US tobacco products. But US tobacco companies still

MOKING
CAUSES
PHYSEM
G WITH EMPHYSEMA
Benson & Hedg
Smooth
SMOKING HARMS
UNBORN BABIES
Quitline
13 7848
Smoking during pregnancy reduces blood flow
placenta and limits the oxygen and nutrients t
growing baby. Smoking increases the risk of
stillbirth, premature birth, problems during th
baby having a smaller brain and body.
You CAN quit smoking. Call Quitline 13 78
doctor or pharmacist, or visit www.quitno
AUSTRALIAN FIRE RISK STANDARD CO
USE CARE IN DISPOSAL.
SMOKI
CAUS
BLINDN
Dunhill
Premier Red

Australia mandates plain branding on cigarette packages accompanied by graphic health warnings.

earn a lot of money. Altria, makers of Marlboro cigarettes, sold $25 billion worth of tobacco products outside the United States and earned $11 billion in profits in 2015.[6]

E-cigs, nicotine patches, antismoking campaigns, strict regulations on smoking in public places, and other factors have steadily pushed down the number of smokers. In response, tobacco companies have diversified their product lines and sought new markets abroad to maintain profits. If other countries begin to follow the American example, however, the international market for tobacco may suffer, and the habit of smoking may die out around the globe.

Tobacco in China

In China, the government-owned China National Tobacco Corporation dominates the market for cigarettes. China National makes Pagoda Mountain and Double Happiness, along with approximately 160 other brands of cigarettes. The largest and most profitable tobacco company in the world, it owns 100 factories, employs 500,000 people, and controls approximately 98 percent of the Chinese market.[7]

The Chinese tobacco industry has also gone high tech. Using a high-speed cigarette-making machine, a single factory in Hongta is capable of producing approximately 90 billion cigarettes every year. The machine, called a Molins Alto, can make 10,000 cigarettes per minute, lowering costs even more for cigarette makers.[8]

TOBACCO PRODUCTION 2013[9]

④ UNITED STATES
381,220 short tons
(345,837 metric tons)

② BRAZIL
937,706 short tons
(850,673 metric tons)

⑧ ARGENTINA
127,133 short tons
(115,334 metric tons)

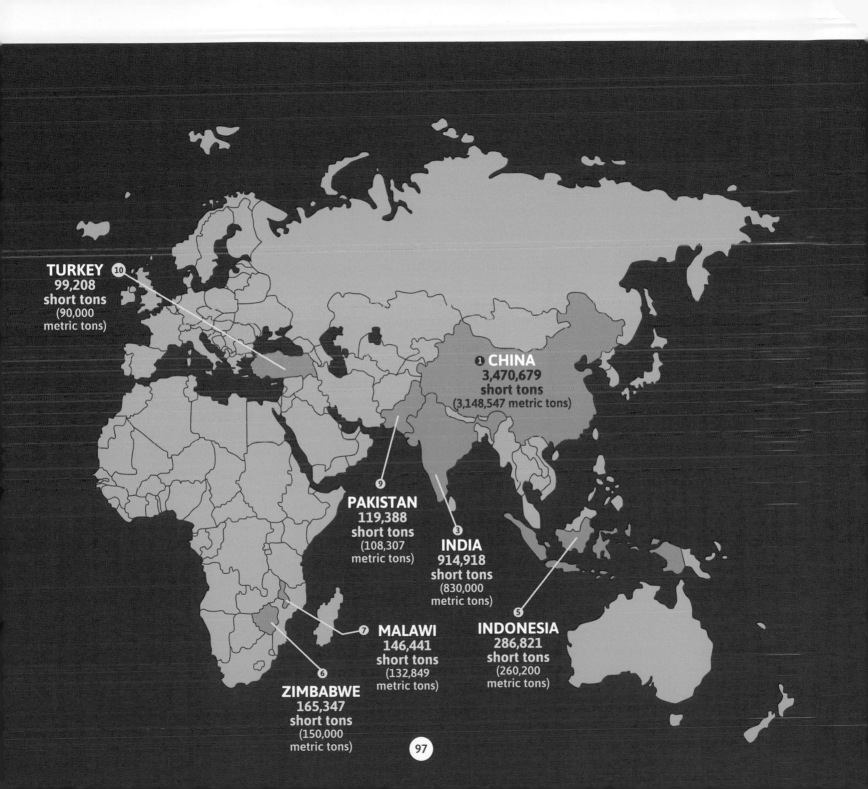

TURKEY ⑩
99,208
short tons
(90,000
metric tons)

❶ **CHINA**
3,470,679
short tons
(3,148,547 metric tons)

⑨

PAKISTAN
119,388
short tons
(108,307
metric tons)

③
INDIA
914,918
short tons
(830,000
metric tons)

⑤

⑦

MALAWI
146,441
short tons
(132,849
metric tons)

INDONESIA
286,821
short tons
(260,200
metric tons)

⑥

ZIMBABWE
165,347
short tons
(150,000
metric tons)

Timeline

1510

Francisco Hernandez de Toledo brings the first tobacco plants from North America to Spain.

1612

John Rolfe of Virginia builds the first tobacco plantation in the English colonies.

1817

Cuba begins exporting tobacco to the United States.

1839

According to legend, Stephen, an enslaved man working on a North Carolina plantation, accidentally discovers bright leaf tobacco.

1850

Reverend George Trask founds the Anti-Tobacco Society.

1864

The federal government imposes its first tax on cigarettes.

1881

James Bonsack patents a complex machine to produce cigarettes.

1890

James Duke founds the American Tobacco Company by merging five separate tobacco firms.

1907

The federal government charges American Tobacco with violating the Sherman Antitrust Act.

1911

The Supreme Court decides against American Tobacco and splits the company into four smaller, independent businesses.

1913

R. J. Reynolds introduces Camel cigarettes, which soon become the country's leading brand.

1921

Iowa becomes the first state to tax cigarettes. By 1969, all 50 states will levy a cigarette tax.

1953

The tobacco industry hires Hill and Knowlton, a public relations firm, to combat medical studies linking cigarette smoking to lung cancer.

1964

The federal government issues the surgeon general's report on smoking and health.

1965

A federal law calls for health warnings to appear on cigarette packs.

1983

Cancer patient Rose Cipollone sues Philip Morris, Lorillard, and Liggett, claiming the companies are responsible for hiding the dangers of cigarettes.

1995

Jeffrey Wigand, a former vice president of Brown and Williamson, agrees to testify against tobacco companies.

1998

Reaching a Master Settlement Agreement, tobacco companies agree to curbs on advertising, to reimburse states for health-care costs, and to fund public antismoking campaigns.

2016

Tobacco companies worldwide produce 24.5 billion cigarettes in the month of April.

Essential Facts

IMPACT ON HISTORY

First cultivated by native peoples of the Americas, tobacco was brought to Europe by explorers and colonists in the 1500s. Its popularity spread, fueling a demand for tobacco plantations in North America. Thanks in part to the labor force of enslaved people used to grow it, it became a profitable crop. By the late 1800s, cigarettes became popular as a way to consume tobacco. Major companies grew so large the US government broke them up. However, concerns about health and morals also drove antismoking campaigns. Still, tobacco companies continued to advertise their products as healthy and glamorous. In the 1950s, definitive scientific evidence about the health dangers of smoking spurred the industry to sow doubt about these risks. These efforts caught up with tobacco companies in the 1990s, when in the United States they were hit with massive lawsuits by customers afflicted with lung cancer and other smoking-related diseases. In the 2000s, smoking has declined in the United States; many companies now work to expand their presence in the international market.

KEY FIGURES

▶ China National Tobacco Corporation is the world's largest and most profitable tobacco business.

▶ Philip Morris International sells Marlboro cigarettes and other brands around the world from its American headquarters.

▶ Whistle-blower Jeffrey Wigand, a former tobacco company vice president, testified about what his company knew about the dangers of cigarette smoke.

▶ Rose Cipollone's lawsuit against several tobacco companies paved the way for other smokers to claim damages for their health problems.

KEY STATISTICS

▸ The annual production of tobacco in the United States totals approximately 800 million pounds (360 million kg).

▸ Approximately 264 billion cigarettes are sold each year in the United States.

▸ Approximately 13 billion cigars are sold each year in the United States.

▸ Approximately 128 million pounds (58 million kg) of smokeless tobacco are sold each year in the United States.

QUOTE

"Washington may be called the head-quarters of tobacco-tinctured saliva. . . . The thing itself is an exaggeration of nastiness, which cannot be outdone."

—*Charles Dickens*

Glossary

carcinogenic

Causing cancer.

e-cigarette

A battery-operated cigarette that creates vapor instead of tobacco smoke (e-cig).

excise tax

A tax charged on the purchase of a specific product.

hopper

A container that is used for storing tobacco in the process of making cigarettes.

lithograph

An image created by a process in which a flat surface is treated to repel ink except where it is required to create the image.

merger

The act of combining two or more companies to create a single, larger one.

monopoly

Exclusive control over a commodity or service.

multinational

A corporation doing business and having offices in more than one country.

nicotine

A chemical compound in tobacco that acts as a stimulant.

snuff

Finely ground tobacco that is placed in the mouth or inhaled.

topping

Removing the flowers that emerge from the tops of tobacco plants to conserve water and energy for the leaves.

trust

An organization formed by several businesses to control prices and the market for goods.

vaping

To inhale and exhale vapor from an electronic cigarette.

whistle-blower

A person who informs authorities about an individual or institution he or she thinks is involved in illegal activity.

Additional Resources

SELECTED BIBLIOGRAPHY

Brandt, Allan. *The Cigarette Century: The Rise, Fall, and Deadly Persistence of the Product that Defined America*. Basic, 2009. Print.

Gately, Ian. *Tobacco: A Cultural History of How an Exotic Plant Seduced Civilization*. Grove, 2001. Print.

Hahn, Barbara. *Making Tobacco Bright: Creating an American Commodity, 1617–1937*. Baltimore, MD: Johns Hopkins UP, 2011. Print.

FURTHER READINGS

Espejo, Roman. *Tobacco and Smoking*. Farmington Hills, MI: Greenhaven, 2015. Print.

Snyder, Gail. *Teens and Smoking*. San Diego, CA: Reference Point, 2015. Print.

WEBSITES

To learn more about Big Business, visit **booklinks.abdopublishing.com**. These links are routinely monitored and updated to provide the most current information available.

FOR MORE INFORMATION

For more information on this subject, contact or visit the following organizations:

Action on Smoking and Health

701 4th Street NW
Washington, DC 20001
202-659-4310
http://www.ash.org

A main focus of this organization is the tracking of antismoking laws and efforts around the world.

American Lung Association

55 W. Wacker Drive, Suite 1150
Chicago, IL 60601
1-800-548-8252
http://www.lung.org

This nonprofit organization researches lung health and lung disease and has been a leading group in the efforts against smoking.

Duke Homestead and Tobacco Factory

2828 Duke Homestead Road
Durham, NC 27705
919-477-5498
http://www.dukehomestead.org

This historic farmstead, with barns and the original factory, is where Washington Duke established his North Carolina tobacco business.

Source Notes

CHAPTER 1. TOBACCO AND NICOTINE

1. Bridgette Steele. "Making Vape at Purebacco." *Northern Express*. Northern Express, 16 Feb. 2015. Web. 28 Sept. 2016.

2. "Excise, 2 May 1794." *Founders Online*. National Archives, n.d. Web. 28 Sept. 2016.

3. "Federal Tobacco Tax Revenues Are Declining." *Tax Foundation*. Tax Foundation, 8 May 2015. Web. 28 Sept. 2016.

CHAPTER 2. TOBACCO IN THE COLONIES

1. Iain Gately. *Tobacco: A Cultural History of How an Exotic Plant Seduced Civilization*. New York: Grove, 2003. Print. 24.

2. "A Counterblaste to Tobacco." *Classic Utilitarianism*. University of Texas at Austin, 24 Sept. 2003. Web. 28 Sept. 2016.

3. "Tobacco Timeline." *Tobacco.org*. Tobacco.org, 25 June 2016. Web. 28 Sept. 2016.

4. Iain Gately. *Tobacco: A Cultural History of How an Exotic Plant Seduced Civilization*. New York: Grove, 2003. Print. 107.

CHAPTER 3. CIGARS, CIGARETTES, AND BRANDS

1. Iain Gately. *Tobacco: A Cultural History of How an Exotic Plant Seduced Civilization*. New York: Grove, 2003. Print. 172.

2. "When Charles Dickens Fell Out with America." *BBC News*. BBC, 14 Feb. 2012. Web. 28 Sept. 2016.

3. "Bright Leaf Tobacco." *Learn NC*. Learn NC, n.d. Web. 28 Sept. 2016.

4. Iain Gately. *Tobacco: A Cultural History of How an Exotic Plant Seduced Civilization*. New York: Grove, 2003. Print. 205.

5. "Sharecropping and Tenant Farming." *Learn NC*. Learn NC, n.d. Web. 28 Sept. 2016.

6. "Duke Homestead State Historic Site." *Duke Homestead State Historic Site and Tobacco Museum*. Duke Homestead, n.d. Web. 28 Sept. 2016.

7. Rich Mueller. "Original Allen & Ginter Baseball Sets Changed Collecting." *Sports Collectors Daily*. Sports Collectors Daily, 15 July 2010. Web. 28 Sept. 2016.

8. Iain Gately. *Tobacco: A Cultural History of How an Exotic Plant Seduced Civilization*. New York: Grove, 2003. Print. 207.

9. "Antitrust History: The American Tobacco Case of 1911." *Foundation for Economic Education*. FEE, 1 Mar. 1971. Web. 28 Sept. 2016.

10. "The Bonsack Machine and Labor Unrest." *Learn NC*. Learn NC, n.d. Web. 22 June 2016.

11. Iain Gately. *Tobacco: A Cultural History of How an Exotic Plant Seduced Civilization*. New York: Grove, 2003. Print. 209.

CHAPTER 4. THE TOBACCO TRUST

1. "The Dukes of Durham." *Learn NC*. Learn NC, n.d. Web. 28 Sept. 2016.

2. "Antitrust History: The American Tobacco Case of 1911." *Foundation for Economic Education*. FEE, 1 Mar. 1971. Web. 28 Sept. 2016.

3. Ibid.

CHAPTER 5. TOBACCO IMAGES

1. Jacob Sullum. *For Your Own Good: The Anti-Smoking Crusade and the Tyranny of Public Health*. New York: Simon, 1999. Print. 25.

2. "Notable and Quotable: Mark Twain on Drinking, Smoking, and 'The Moral Statistician.'" *Wall Street Journal*. Wall Street Journal, n.d. Web. 28 Sept. 2016.

3. Carl Sferrazza Anthony. "Our Presidents and Cigars." *Cigar Aficionado*. Cigar Aficionado, Autumn 1993. Web. 28 Sept. 2016.

4. "Camel Cigarettes." *North Carolina History Project*. North Carolina History, n.d. Web. 5 June 2016.

5. Ibid.

6. Wendy Christensen. "Torches of Freedom: Women and Smoking Propaganda." *Sociological Images*. Society Pages, 27 Feb. 2012. Web. 28 Sept. 2016.

7. Elizabeth Crisp Crawford. *Tobacco Goes to College: Cigarette Advertising in Student Media, 1920-1980*. Jefferson, NC: McFarland, 2014. Print. 189.

8. Chris Harrald and Fletcher Watkins. *The Cigarette Book: The History and Culture of Smoking*. New York: Skyhorse, 2010. Print. 161.

9. Liz Emanuel. "State Cigarette Tax Rates in 2014." *Tax Foundation*. Tax Foundation, 2 July 2014. Web. 28 Sept. 2016.

CHAPTER 6. THE CIGARETTE AGE

1. "Smoke Gets in Your Eyes: 20th Century Tobacco Advertisements." *National Museum of American History*. Smithsonian, 17 Mar. 2014. Web. 28 Sept. 2016.

2. Chris Harrald and Fletcher Watkins. *The Cigarette Book: The History and Culture of Smoking*. New York: Skyhorse, 2010. Print. 145.

3. "Second Hand Smoke Facts." *CDC*. CDC, n.d. Web. 28 Sept. 2016.

4. Will Storr. "The Quest to Create the Cancer-Free Cigarette Continues." *Business Insider*. Business Insider, 6 Sept. 2012. Web. 28 Sept. 2016.

5. Michael J. Goodman. "Tobacco's PR Campaign: The Cigarette Papers." *Los Angeles Times*. Los Angeles Times, 18 Sept. 1994. Web. 27 June 2016.

6. Myron Levin. "Remember When Big Tobacco Sold Asbestos as the 'Greatest Health Protection'?" *Mother Jones*. Mother Jones, 22 Oct. 2013. Web. 26 June 2016.

7. "Scarface (1932)." *TCM*. TCM, 2016. Web. 28 Sept. 2016.

8. "Smoke Gets in Your Eyes: 20th Century Tobacco Advertisements." *National Museum of American History*. Smithsonian, 17 Mar. 2014. Web. 28 Sept. 2016.

Source Notes Continued

CHAPTER 7. TOBACCO IN COURT

1. "Required Warnings for Cigarette Packages and Advertisements." *Federal Register*. Federal Register, 12 Nov. 2010. Web. 16 June 2016.

2. Allan M. Brandt. *The Cigarette Century*. New York: Basic, 2007. Print. 325.

3. "Inside the Tobacco Deal." *Frontline*. PBS, 2014. Web. 27 June 2016.

4. Rick Lyman. "A Tobacco Whistle-Blower's Life Is Transformed." *New York Times*. New York Times, 15 Oct. 1999. Web. 28 Sept. 2016.

5. Kathleen Michon. "Tobacco Litigation History and Development." *NOLO*. NOLO, 30 Dec. 2015. Web. 28 Sept. 2016.

6. "Master Settlement Agreement." *Public Health Law Center*. Mitchell Hamline School of Law, 2016. Web. 28 Sept. 2016.

7. Kathleen Michon. "Tobacco Litigation History and Development." *NOLO*. NOLO, 30 Dec. 2015. Web. 28 Sept. 2016.

8. "*Engle v. Liggett Group Inc*." *FindLaw*. FindLaw, 2016. Web. 28 Sept. 2016.

9. Alexandra Sifferlin. "Teen Smoking Is Way Down, But What About E-Cigs?" *Time*. Time, 12 June 2014. Web. 22 June 2016.

CHAPTER 8. THE TOBACCO BUSINESS

1. "Statistical Report – Tobacco." *Alcohol and Tobacco Trade and Tax Bureau*. Department of the Treasury, Apr. 2016. Web. 28 Sept. 2016.

2. "Grades and Standards: Flue-Cured Tobacco." *USDA*. USDA, n.d. Web. 15 June 2016.

3. "The 2016 Forecast for Tobacco." *Convenience Store News*. Convenience Store News, 18 Jan. 2016. Web. 28 Sept. 2016.

4. W. Kip Viscusi. "Smoked Out." *U of Chicago P*. U of Chicago P, n.d. Web. 28 Sept. 2016.

5. Liz Emanuel. "State Cigarette Tax Rates in 2014." *Tax Foundation*. Tax Foundation, 2 July 2014. Web. 28 Sept. 2016.

6. "Company Overview." *Philip Morris*. Philip Morris International, n.d. Web. 15 June 2016.

7. Aaron Smith. "60% of Cigarettes in New York Are Smuggled: Report." *CNN*. CNN, 1 Jan. 2013. Web. 21 June 2016.

8. "About Philip Morris USA." *Altria*. Altria, n.d. Web. 28 Sept. 2016.

9. "Standardised Tobacco Packaging." *Smokefree Action*. Smokefree Action, n.d. 15 June 2016.

10. Kadhim Shubber. "Tobacco Looks to Gain in Developing World Despite Cancer." *Financial Times*. Financial Times, 2 June 2016. Web. 15 June 2016.

11. Judy Peres. "No Clear Link Between Passive Smoking and Lung Cancer." *Journal of the National Cancer Institute*. National Cancer Institute, 5 Dec. 2013. Web. 26 June 2016.

12. "Bain et al. vs Philip Morris." *SmokeLitigation.org*. Public Health Advocacy Institute, 2016. Web. 4 Aug. 2016.

13. "Smoking Ban on Planes: November 21, 1989." *Health Central*. Health Central, 2015. Web. 27 June 2016.

CHAPTER 9. NEW MARKETS, NEW PRODUCTS

1. "Reynolds American – Form 10K." *US Securities and Exchange Commission*. SEC, March 2016. Web. 17 June 2016.

2. "Our Products and Ingredients." *Altria*. Altria, n.d. Web. 18 June 2016.

3. "Trends in Current Cigarette Smoking among High School Students and Adults, 1965–2014." *Centers for Disease Control and Prevention*. CDC, n.d. Web. 27 June 2016.

4. "The Global Cigarette Industry." *Campaign for Tobacco-Free Kids*. Campaign for Tobacco-Free Kids, Sept. 2015. Web. 18 June 2016.

5. Te-Ping Chen. "China's Marlboro Country." *Slate*. Slate, 29 June 2009. Web. 22 June 2016.

6. "Altria Group: Income Statement." *Yahoo Finance*. Yahoo, 27 June 2016. Web. 27 June 2016.

7. Andrew Martin. "The Chinese Government Is Getting Rich Selling Cigarettes." *Bloomberg*. Bloomberg, 12 Dec. 2014. Web. 18 June 2016.

8. "Alto." *Molins Tobacco Machinery*. Molins PLC, 2016. Web. 28 Sept. 2016.

9. "Download Data." *Food and Agriculture Organization of the United Nations Statistics Division*. FAOSTAT, 2015. Web. 28 Sept. 2016.

Index

ABOUT THE AUTHOR

Tom Streissguth has written more than 100 nonfiction books for young people. He has worked as a journalist, teacher, and editor, and he is the founder of the Archive of American Journalism, which publishes long-neglected works of authors such as Mark Twain, Jack London, and Ernest Hemingway. He lives in Woodbury, Minnesota.